Creating Applications with Microsoft Access 2010

Revised (print) edition publication date June 16, 2014

Digital rights provided by agreement to

Amazon Digital Services, Inc.

Print rights provided by agreement to

CreateSpace, an Amazon company

by best-selling e-book author
Edward Jones

Access®, Excel®, and Windows® are registered trademarks of Microsoft Corporation.

Visual Basic is a trademark of Microsoft Corporation.

Oracle® is a registered trademark of Oracle Corporation.

Introduction

You are well past the basics; you are the expert that others look to when they need help getting the job done with Microsoft Access. Now, take your database skills to the next level! In this book, you will learn how you can-

• Design your database tables and relationships for maximum effectiveness

• Learn the secrets of parameter query design to get the data you need on demand

• Design forms and reports that display and summarize data precisely as it is needed

• Put it all together by creating complete applications that others can use with no specialized Access training

Building Applications with Microsoft Access 2010 is a get-it-done guide for developing complete custom applications using Microsoft Access, the world's most popular Windows-based database management software. Microsoft Access is the corporate standard for creating desktop database solutions. If you are a power user who serves as the 'office guru' for everyday users of Access, or a developer for a corporate or government agency who must gain a familiarity with Access as a development platform for applications, As a database management system and a strong development environment combined into a single package, Microsoft Access is the corporate standard for creating desktop database solutions. If you are a power user who serves as the 'office guru' for everyday users of Access, or a developer for a corporate or government agency who must gain a familiarity with Access as a development platform for applications, you'll find this book to be a must-read.

This book is designed for experienced Microsoft Access users who are learning to develop applications for

the first time, and for experienced programmers who are moving to Microsoft Access from another development system. You'll get the most from this book if you are already familiar with the basic capabilities of Access, such as creating tables and queries, and designing forms and reports.

Table of Contents

Introduction 3
Table of Contents 5
Chapter 1 - Why Develop Applications Using Access? 7
Access applications, defined 9
Chapter 2 - Building Blocks of an Access App 13
Connecting the dots 17
Getting a fast start to database development with Access
templates 18
Chapter 3 - Your First Access App, a Hands-On Example
.... 21
Chapter 4 - Laying a Solid Foundation with Table
Relationships 37
Chapter 5 - Fast Application Development with the
Command Button Wizard 45
Setting the Access Options for Your Application 48
Chapter 6 - Putting It All Together 51
Navigating Between Forms of an Application 51
Displaying Message Boxes with Macros or VBA 53
Getting Input for Programming Tasks 55
Providing Users with Help 56
Creating a Shortcut to Launch the Application 57
Chapter 7 - Recommendations for User Interface Design 59
Summary 65

Chapter 1 - Why Develop Applications Using Access?

Access stands out as the most popular database management system available for Windows-based computers. If you are faced with a 'buy' decision for a desktop database management system, no real competition to Access exists in terms of market share. And market share is important, as it directly translates to a wide base of third-party support. You can readily find books, inexpensive training courses (in classrooms and on the web), and third-party add-ons to support any development project using Access.

With database applications, true alternatives to Access as a choice of development platform come from other products aimed at providing enterprise-wide solutions, or development (i.e., programming) languages. Included in such alternatives are Java, Visual Basic, and Visual C++. Using any of these products, you can develop Windows-based front ends that allow you to add, query, and report on data stored in back-end databases like Microsoft SQL Server, Oracle, and Sybase. The advantage of using Access over these offerings is that Access can stand alone as both a front-end development tool, and as a complete desktop database management solution. Access also offers a moderate learning curve when compared to the steeper learning curves of pure programming languages like Java, Visual C++, or Visual Basic. And with Access, the time to develop applications is greatly reduced when compared to development tools like Visual Basic, Java, or Visual C++.

The primary disadvantage of Access when viewed as a development tool for database management can be the cost of deployment. Since an Access license is required for each user, the price of deploying an Access application on a wide scale could become prohibitively expensive.

As a pure database management solution, Access does have its limits. If your application will involve hundreds of thousands or millions of records, or dozens of simultaneous data-entry personnel, you likely will not be happy with the limitations of Access. In theory, Access can handle databases with millions of records, and an unlimited number of simultaneous connections. But in practice, performance suffers when databases grow to massive sizes. And any enterprise-wide database solution will also require the security and scalability that you can only achieve from a robust server-based product like Microsoft's SQL Server or Oracle. However, even in cases where workload demands necessitate the use of SQL Server or Oracle as database management standards, you should not discount the use of Access. Databases like SQL Server and Oracle are databases, but they are not front-end development tools. So, even if you place your data on a server like the above, you must still choose a tool to provide end users with the interface they need to add data, perform queries, and produce reports. Again, Access can meet this need, as it is also designed to act as the front end or 'client' in a client/server database solution.

Given that the same company is behind both Microsoft SQL Server and Access, it is no surprise that Access works best with Microsoft SQL Server. However, you can use Access as a front end to Oracle and Sybase databases as well. Incidentally, if you are planning to use Access as a front end to a database stored on Microsoft's SQL Server, you can find a wealth of information about this topic at the Microsoft web site. Go to www.microsoft.com/access, under 'Meet the Access Community' click the 'Developers' link, and at the next page, from the links at the left sidebar click the 'Access Visual How-Tos' link, and peruse the articles you will find listed.

Access applications, defined

The ultimate goal of any Access application is to make database management a simple task for users. Scratch beneath the surface and it becomes apparent that the application accomplishes nothing that end users could not accomplish with Access on their own, given sufficient training. The need for an application arises when you ask the question, how much training do you want to devote to users to enable them to perform a specific set of database management tasks?

If you analyze the demands of any given database management task and then examine an actual database created by a user to perform that task, you will see a group of Access *objects* that have been created to work in concert to meet a particular need. These objects include the following:

tables containing records of doctors and patients, or lawyers and clients, or customers and sales

queries that enable the end users of the database to retrieve specific sets of records, such as all sales completed by a given sales representative within a specific month

forms designed to speed data entry, and to enable users to find, display, and edit (or delete) a given record stored within a table

reports to summarize the data stored within the database, and to print data in specific formats such as sales histories, patient visitation records, or invoices

All of these objects alone comprise a database. And if your end user is experienced in the use of Access, he or she will use the various Access objects, on an interactive basis, to get their jobs done. Users can open forms and use the built-in Access menus to search for records, design and run queries as needed, and create reports to make use of the tables and queries stored within the database. Problem is, such interactive use of Access requires a reasonable familiarity with the product. If end users are to be expected to accomplish tasks like these, they must be reasonably familiar with the use of Access (on an interactive basis) as are you, dear reader. How much time do you (or your help desk staff) wish to devote to training end users in the complexities of query design, mapping reports to queries that they create, and launching the correct Access objects from within the Navigation Pane? And, when an experienced Access user leaves the organization, do you want to repeat the process again with the new employee who has been hired as a replacement?

Assuming that the answer to the above question is an emphatic *no*, then you want to progress from the above scenario (which uses nothing more than an Access database) to a fully-designed Access application. In a nutshell, the difference between an Access database and an Access application boils down to ease-of-use. Access applications are complete, working systems designed for novice users. Such applications provide menus or "switchboards" containing clearly-defined user options that guide users (who may have little or no knowledge of the inner workings of Microsoft Access) through specific database management tasks. As an example, Figure 1 shows the main menu of an Access application designed to handle marketing for a large law firm. If an end user can double-click a desktop icon and immediately view a form like this one, with customized options that lead to other forms and shield the user from the inner workings of Microsoft Access, the user is making use of a complete application.

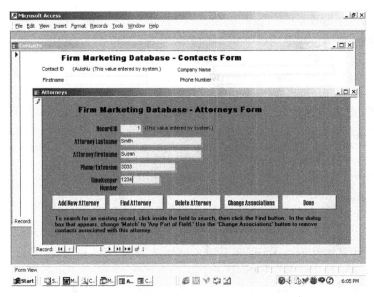

Figure 1 An example of an Access application

The Database Templates that Access can download from Office.com generate moderately complex applications with little or no design work on your part. However, the major limitation to the Database Templates is that they can only produce databases for the specific tasks shown in the list of available databases. If your data management task falls outside that realm (as is so often the case), you must design your own applications within Access to provide users with an equally-friendly interface. And the tasks behind designing such applications is what this book will cover in detail.

You can think of an Access application as a set of Access objects designed to handle a specific database management task, with a shield wrapped around these objects to hide many of them from the end user. Any application will contain certain objects that users see (such as forms, reports, and custom menus) along with objects that the user never sees directly, but are nevertheless integral parts of the application. These hidden objects typically include the underlying tables, queries, and any

11

macros and VBA 'procedures' or program code. When you develop a complete Access application, you design the basic objects using the design features of Access, and you add a user interface designed around the use of forms and custom menus. As needed, you modify the default behavior of the Access objects, using macros and VBA code as necessary.

Another important reason for designing and implementing a complete Access application is to provide a form of security for the database. In the hands of a less-than-proficient user, the power inherent in Microsoft Access can be a dangerous thing. Without safeguards, users can make massive unwanted changes to tables, break the design of queries, modify reports in ways that no longer produce desired results, and even delete needed tables. If you want to safeguard your databases from such user-induced horrors, you will need to create custom applications that keep your users safely apart from the inner workings of Access.

Chapter 2 - Building Blocks of an Access App

Access *forms* comprise the fundamental means of interaction between an Access database and your end users. Forms provide the means for users to view, add, and edit data. Additionally, as a developer, they provide you with a means of quickly implementing a user interface. In reality (as far as the user is concerned), the forms *are* the application, because the forms are what the user sees from the time that Access opens the database until the user exits from the system.

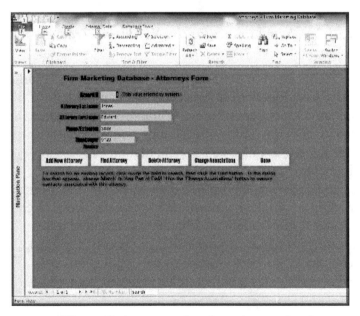

Figure 2 An example of an Access form

A common use for forms in designing custom applications is to use them as *home screens*, which serve as starting points that allow users to reach the various parts of your application. As an example, you can download the Northwind Traders 2007 database (the sample database that is provided at Office.com), and open the form titled **Home**. The form that appears (Figure 3) is an example of a home screen. You can design forms with command buttons that open other forms for data entry and editing, or open or print reports or perform other common end user tasks.

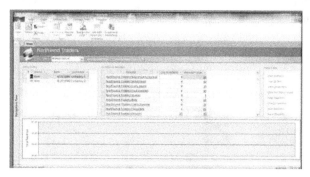

Figure 3 The home screen for the Northwind Traders 2007 database

At the heart of your database, *tables* (Figure 4) form the underlying source of information that is provided through any Access application. While this book assumes a familiarity with the basics of designing and working with Access tables, it is important to note that the process of creating tables involves more than simply entering the names and choosing appropriate data types. Because you are creating a complete application to meet the needs of end users, careful forethought and planning is required before you create your tables. If your tables are poorly designed, they can hinder the performance of the application, and make daily processes much more difficult for your end users.

Figure 4 An example of a typical Access table

When designing any application, you will want to apply the steps of *normalization* (the elimination of unnecessary duplication of data) to the implementation of your underlying tables. (This step is particularly important if you are creating an application based on data that has been exported from a spreadsheet such as Microsoft Excel. It is possible to store massive amounts of data in Excel, but it is not always done in an efficient manner. And since Excel does not possess true relational capabilities, many users store data with unnecessary duplication of information.)

In addition to tables, *queries* (Figure 5) form another vital building block in the typical Access application. They are necessary for retrieving selective data from your tables, and for retrieving data in a specific order. The forms and reports in a typical Access application often make direct use of queries as a data source. This is a vital concept for any beginning Access developer to grasp, as it can significantly reduce the time needed to develop complex applications.

As an example, perhaps you are designing a database application to manage an extensive mailing list of

15

clients, and your users wish to produce mailing labels by city, by the office responsible for the client, or by Zip code group. Within Access, you could create a single report to generate the mailing labels in the format desired. You could then use the Edit/Copy command to create additional copies of that report under different names, and then set the Record Source property for each report to a different query in order to produce the desired labels. The step-by-step example of a simple yet complete Access application (provided in the hands-on example in the next chapter) includes a demonstration of this design technique.

And while we are on the subject of queries, it is worth noting that parameter queries can be an application developer's best friend when it comes to fast retrieval of data that varies on a case-by-case basis. Parameter queries are a common topic of intermediate Access use, but if you are unfamiliar with the design of such, browse the Help files in Access and learn how to design and build these objects.

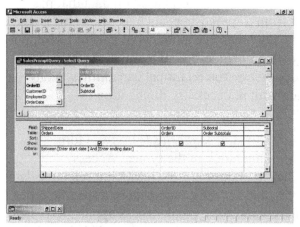

Figure 5 The design of a typical parameter query

Reports (Figure 6) round out the collection of the "basic four" objects used within an Access database, and these can be quickly designed, manually or with the aid of the Report Wizards, to produce your data in a format needed by users of the application.

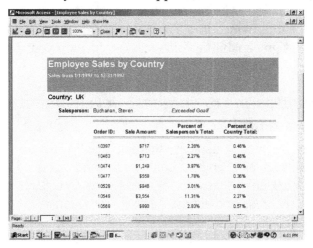

Figure 6 An example of an Access report

Connecting the dots

Once you have a complete collection of Access objects that an experienced Access user could work with on an interactive basis to perform a given data management task, you are only partially finished with the application design process. You still must bind them together underneath a user interface- a process of "connecting the dots," so to speak- to provide a working application for your end users. You do this by creating any command buttons, macros, and VBA code needed to open or run the various objects within your application.

As an example, a home form button, created with the aid of the Command Button Wizards (discussed later in this book), could contain VBA code that opens and prints a report. The report may use a parameter query as its data source. The expression within the Criteria cell of the parameter query would prompt the end user for the criteria that controls what subset of records appears in the report. In this example, the parameter query is directly linked to the report, and the report is linked (by means of VBA code) to

17

the button on the home screen or. It is this process of connecting the various Access objects that makes for a complete application. And once you grasp how Access objects can be intertwined into a complete application, you can use the design capabilities of Access to develop your own custom applications.

Getting a fast start to database development with Access templates

When the type of database that you need serves an everyday task such as keeping a contacts list, managing projects, keeping up with events, or tracking to-do tasks, you can quickly create a database that is based upon a *template*. A template is a model that, when opened, creates a complete Access application. The application already contains all the table relationships, queries, forms, reports, and VBA programming code that is needed to meet your specific tasks. The full installation of Access 2010 comes with five web database templates and seven client database templates. The client databases are designed to be saved to a shared network location, and multiple users can then simultaneously work with the databases. The web databases are designed to be used with a Microsoft SharePoint server that supports Access Services. (You can also use any of the web databases as client databases, saving any one of these databases on a shared network drive where multiple users can use the database.)

To create a database that's based on a template, use these steps:

1. On the File tab, click New.

2. Under Available Templates near the center of the screen, click Sample Templates to display a collection of sample database templates. These include ready-to-use databases for the following tasks:

Assets Tracking

18

Charitable Contributions (web-enabled)

Contacts (web-enabled)

Events

Faculty

Issues Tracking (web-enabled)

Marketing Projects (web-enabled)

Projects

Students

Tasks

Alternately, in the Office.com area of the screen you can click any of the templates shown, or you can double-click one of the category folders shown to see all available templates within that category. Double-click any of the templates that appears to meet your need, and Access will create a new database based upon that template.

Hint: *If you are looking to create a database for a very specific task—say, "real estate listings"-- and you don't see that task listed in the Office.com templates area, you can enter a search term, such as "real estate" in the 'Search Office.com Templates box. Any templates at the Microsoft Office.com web site matching the search term will be downloaded to your computer. (This assumes you have a live internet connection.)*

Note: *Many of the templates at Office.com are not produced by Microsoft, but are instead provided by third party vendors. They appear to be well-designed and clearly had to meet certain quality standards to be included on the Microsoft web site, but Microsoft certainly makes no guarantees that a particular template will accomplish all that you want from the resulting database.*

Chapter 3 - Your First Access App, a Hands-On Example

There is no substitute for real-world experience, so the following portion of this article offers a step-by-step example of application development using Access 2010 or 2007. Before performing the steps, you will need to create two small tables. One, named *Clients*, contains a listing of client names for a sales organization. The second table, named *Calls*, contains a record of each telephone call made by a sales rep to a particular client. Table 1 shows the table structure for the Clients table, with sample data following the design. Table 2 shows the structure for the Calls table, with sample data following the design. A one-to-many relationship exists between the Clients table and the Calls table, as shown in Figure 7. (You can use the Relationships button in the Database Tools portion of the ribbon to create this relationship between the tables.)

Figure 7 The Relationships window containing the Clients and Calls tables

Table 1 Clients

Field name	Data type
ClientID	Text (This field should be a key field.)

Last name	Text
First name	Text
Address	Text
City	Text
State	Text
Zip	Text
Phone	Text

After you create the Clients table with the above structure, open the new table in Datasheet view, and enter the following four sample records.

(Sample data for the Clients table:)

ClientID	101
Lastname	Smith
Firstname	Linda
Address	101 Main St.
City	Annapolis
State	MD
Zip	20711
Phone	301 555-4032

ClientID	102
Lastname	Johnson
Firstname	Steven
Address	452 Apple Way

City	Washington
State	DC
Zip	20005
Phone	202 555-3090

ClientID	103
Lastname	O'Malley
Firstname	Susan
Address	1905 Park Ave.
City	New York
State	NY
Zip	10014
Phone	212 555-7879

ClientID	104
Lastname	Bannerman
Firstname	David
Address	434 Ocean Dr.
City	Miami
State	FL
Zip	29101
Phone	308 555-2037

(Table 2 - Calls table)

Field name	Data type
ClientID	Text
CallDate	Date/time
CallTime	Date/Time
Comments	Memo

After you create the Calls table with the above structure, open the new table in Datasheet view, and enter the following five sample records.

(Sample data for the Calls table:)

ClientID	101
CallDate	2/15/12
CallTime	9:30 AM
Comments	Schedule shipment of CD101 drives.

ClientID	101
CallDate	2/17/12
CallTime	11:00 AM
Comments	Confirm receipt of CD101 shipment.

ClientID	102
CallDate	2/15/12
CallTime	3:30 PM

Comments	Arrange credit for retail store.

ClientID	104
CallDate	2/16/12
CallTime	10:20 AM
Comments	Customer call re: quality control issues.

ClientID	104
CallDate	2/17/12
CallTime	2:15 PM
Comments	Follow-up to call of 2/16.

1. Once both tables and the relationship between the tables have been created and the sample records have been added to both tables, in the Navigation Pane at the left, choose Tables, and click Clients to select this table.

2 In the menu bar area (at the top of the screen), click the Create tab. Then under Forms, click Form Wizard to display the Form Wizard dialog box (Figure 8).

Figure 8 First dialog of the Form Wizard dialog box

3. Click the double-arrow button (>>) to move all the fields from the Clients table into the form. Then under Tables/Queries in the dialog box, open the drop-down and choose Calls. Again, click the double-arrow button (>>) to move all of the fields from the Calls table onto the form, and click Next.

4. The next screen of the Form Wizard that appears (Figure 9) will ask how you want to view the data, by Clients, or by Calls.

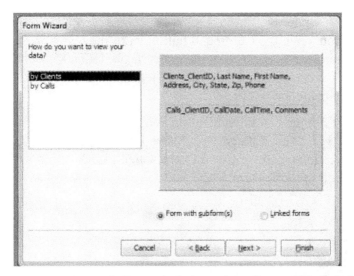

Figure 9 Second dialog of the Form Wizard dialog box

5. Leave the default values as-is, and click Finish. Access will create a default form that displays the clients within the main part of the form, and the calls for each client within a subform (Figure 10).

Figure 10 Completed form created by the Form Wizard

6. Right-click the Clients tab for the form (at the top left of the form itself), and choose Design View from the pop-up menu that appears. This action changes the form's appearance from form view to design view.

7. Under the Form Design Tools area now visible in the ribbon, click the Command button icon (the one resembling a rectangle containing a series of letter X's). Then click on a blank space within the right side of the form, to place the button.

8. In the Command Button Wizard dialog box (Figure 11), under Categories, choose **Form Operations**. Under Actions, choose **Close Form**. Click Finish to add a Close button to the form.

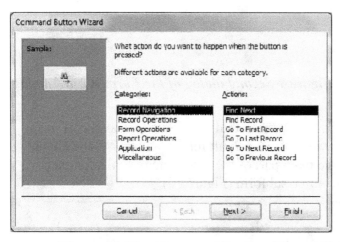

Figure 11 The Command Button Wizard dialog box

9. Save and close the form, and accept the default name of **Clients**.

10. With the Clients table still selected in the Navigation Pane, and the Create tab still active in the ribbon area (at the top of the screen), click Report Wizard. The first dialog box for the Report Wizard appears (Figure 12).

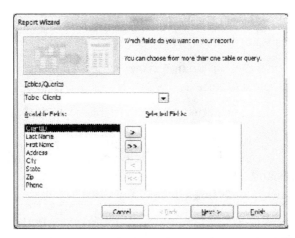

Figure 12 First dialog of the Report Wizard dialog box

11. In the Available Fields portion of the dialog box, double-click the Last Name, First Name, City, and Phone fields.

12. In the Tables/Queries list box within the same dialog box, select the Calls table.

13. In the Available Fields box, double-click the CallDate, CallTime, and Comments fields.

14. In the Report Wizard dialog box, click Finish. Access will create a default report showing each client along with the phone calls made to that client. (In Design View, you may need to widen the CallDate and CallTime fields to get the data to display properly.)

15. Save and close the new report, and in the Navigation Pane, rename the report to **AllCalls**. (To do this, right-click the report in the Navigation Pane, choose Rename from the pop-up menu that appears, and type the new name for the report.)

Next, you will design a *parameter query* that supports the reporting of calls for a range of dates, and you will create a copy of an existing report to be used with the parameter query. Use the following steps to accomplish these design tasks:

1. In the Navigation Pane, under All Access Objects, select Queries.

2. In the ribbon area, under Create, click Query Design.

3. In the Show Table dialog box, double-click both the Calls and Clients tables to add both tables to the design of the query, and click Close to put away the dialog box.

4. In the Clients field list (in the upper portion of the query design window), click the first field to select it, hold the Shift key depressed and click the last field in the list to select all the fields, and click and drag the fields as a group to the first empty column in the query design grid.

5. Scroll to the right within the query design grid and locate the next empty column. Then, in the Calls field list (in the upper portion of the query design window), click the CallDate field, hold the Shift key depressed, and click the Comments field to select the CallDate, CallTime, and Comments fields simultaneously. Then click and drag these fields as a group to the next empty column in the query grid.

6. Locate the CallDate field that was added to the design of the query. In the Criteria row for the CallDate field, type the following expression (including the left and right bracket characters):

Between [Enter starting date:] and [Enter ending date:]

7. Save and close the query. When prompted for a name, call the query **CallsByDate**.

8. In the Navigation Pane, change the object type to Reports, to display the existing reports.

9. Right-click the **AllCalls** report and from the popup menu that appears, choose Copy

10. Right-click in any blank portion of the Navigation Pane, and choose **Paste** from the pop-up menu that appears, to create a copy of the report.

11. When asked for a report name, enter **CallsByDate**.

12. In the Navigation Pane, right-click the CallsByDate report and choose Design to open the CallsByDate report in Design view.

13. If the Properties sheet isn't already visible at the far right, click Property Sheet in the ribbon area to display the Property Sheet for the report..

14. Click the Data tab within the Properties sheet.

15. Click the Down Arrow to the right of the Record Source property, and choose CallsByDate from the list. (This action links the new report to the parameter query that you created earlier.)

16. Save the changes to the report, and close the report.

With these objects (two tables, one query, one form with a subform, and two reports) created, you can proceed to create a home screen based on a form that presents a friendly user interface to the end user. As mentioned, home screens are simply blank forms with command buttons added that perform various tasks (such as opening a form or printing a report). The buttons that you place on the blank form can use VBA code (usually added with the aid of the Command Button Wizards) or Access macros to perform common tasks. By way of example, try the following steps to create a home screen for the application:

1. In the ribbon area, under Create, click Blank Form..

31

2. Right-click the tab of the new form that appears, and choose Design view from the pop-up menu.

3. Using typical Access form design techniques, size the blank form so that it measures roughly four inches square.

4. In the ribbon area, under Form Design Tools, select the Design tab if it isn't already highlighted

5. In the ribbon area, click the Button icon to select the Command Button tool.

6. Click near the center of the form, roughly one inch below the top of the form to start the Command Button Wizard.

7. Under Categories, choose Form Operations. Under Actions, choose Open Form, and click Next.

8. In the next dialog box that appears, select **Clients** as the form to open, then click Next.

9. In the next dialog box, leave the default choice of 'Open the form and show all the records' selected, and click Next.

10. In the next dialog box, click Text, and enter 'Add or Edit Records' in the text dialog box, then click Finish.

11. In the ribbon area, click the Command Button tool to select it.

12. Click roughly one-half inch below the button you created previously, to start the Command Button Wizard.

13. Under Categories, select Report Operations. Under Actions, select Preview Report, then click Next.

14. In the list that appears in the next dialog box, leave the default of **AllCalls** selected in the list, and click Next.

15. In the next dialog box, click Text, enter 'All Calls Report' in the text box, and then click Finish.

16. In the ribbon area, click the Command Button tool to select it.

17. Click roughly one-half inch below the button you created previously, to start the Command Button Wizard.

18. Under Categories, select Report Operations. Under Actions, select Preview Report, then click Next.

19. In the list that appears in the next dialog box, select **CallsByDate** in the list, and click Next.

20. In the next dialog box, click Text, enter 'Calls by Date Report' in the text box, and then click Finish.

21. In the ribbon area, click the Command Button tool to select it.

22. Click roughly one-half inch below the button you created previously, to start the Command Button Wizard.

24. Under Categories, select Application. Under Actions, leave the default choice of Quit Application selected, and click Next.

25. In the next dialog box, click Text, enter 'Exit System' in the text box, and click Finish.

26. Click above and to the left of the first button, and drag to the lower right of the last button. When you release the mouse, all the buttons should appear selected.

27. Right-click any of the selected buttons and choose Align Left, then right-click any selected button and choose Size/To Widest from the menus.

32. Click the Label tool in the ribbon area, then click and drag near the top of the form to create a new label roughly three inches wide and one-half inch high.

33. Type the heading **Client Calls Tracking System** in the label, and change the font of the label to 16-point type. (You can select the label, then use the Properties Sheet at the far right to change the font.)

34. Click any blank spot in the form to select the entire form. In the ribbon area, click the Property Sheet icon, if it isn't already visible.

35. Click the Format tab of the Property Sheet. In the options that appear, set the Scroll Bars option to Neither, the Record Selectors option to No, the Navigation Buttons option to No, and the Auto Center option to Yes.

36. Save and close the form. When asked for a name, call the form **Home**.

Finally, you can set startup options for the database (these are explained in more detail under the heading that follows). Use these steps to do this, completing the design of this simple application:

1. In the main menu bar area at the top of the screen, click the File tab.

2. Under Help, click Options.

3. In the Access Options dialog box that appears (Figure 13), click Current Database.

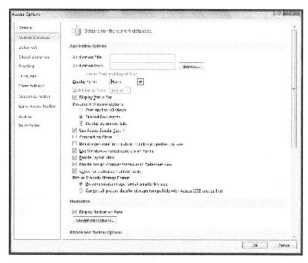

Figure 13 The Access Options dialog box

4. In the Display Form drop-down, choose Home as the screen you want the application to initially display.

5. Turn off the option to Display Navigation Panel, then click OK.

6. Choose File > Close Database to close the database

At this point, the simple application is complete. If you close the database and re-open it, the home screen appears, similar to the example shown in Figure 14. From here, users can perform common database tasks with little or no specific knowledge of Microsoft Access.

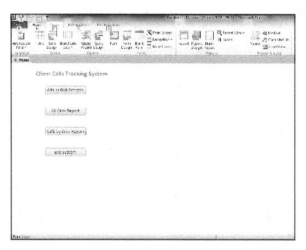

Figure 14 The example home screen

While this example has been kept intentionally simple for the sake of brevity, you can utilize the same techniques with any custom Access application. If your application has a variety of forms and reports (as most do), you can have one form open another from to keep the user interface manageable. For example, a 'Reports' button on your home screen might open another form that contains buttons used to print a variety of reports.

Chapter 4 - Laying a Solid Foundation with Table Relationships

One important difference that sets an Access application developer apart from the experienced Access user involves the planning and implementation of the table structure used for the application. The creation of tables, with their various field names and field types, involves basic skills that anyone who has been using Access for any length of time should be familiar with. However, database developers must move beyond such basic skills, and include the relationships between multiple tables, and the need for *referential integrity*, as an integral part of the development process. Since the majority of complex database applications (and *all* truly 'relational' applications) will involve the use of more than one table, the relationship between all tables within a database will have an effect on relational queries and subsequent forms and reports, and hence, on many parts of the design and implementation of the overall application.

Part of the process of designing tables for Access applications involves the selection of an appropriate field or combination of fields to be used as the *primary key* within the table. A primary key is a field or combination of fields that serves to uniquely identify every record within a table. While Access does not require the addition of a primary key to any table, one is necessary to establish a relationship between the table and another (related) table. For example, consider the simple case of the clients and calls tables used in the hands-on example described earlier. This example demonstrates the *one-to-many* relationship, commonly found in most database applications. In the example, the Clients table contains the names, addresses, and phone numbers of various clients of a sales organization. A second table, Calls, contains a listing of all phone calls made to a particular client. Each record in the Clients table (which represents a single client) can be related to one or more records in the Calls table. The result is a one-to-many relationship between the Clients table and the Calls table. And in this example, the relationship between the tables is based on the ClientID field, which is a primary key in the Clients table, and a foreign key in the Calls table. Since no two clients can have the same ClientID number, the ClientID field uniquely identifies every client in the Clients table.

Entire books have been written on the subject of relational database planning and we won't belabor the point here. But suffice to say that if you plan to develop applications within Access, you should be familiar with the various types of relationships that can be created. Access (along with nearly all database managers used by personal computers) supports three types of relationships: *one-to-one*, *one to-many*, and *many-to-many*. The terms refer to the number of records found in the initial, or "parent" table, that can be related to the number of records found in the related, or "child" table. In the hands-on example, since one client can have any number of phone calls made to that client, a one-to-many relationship exists between the Clients table and the Calls table. This is by far the most common type of relationship you will need in your Access applications.

Less commonly, you will encounter one-to-one and many-to-many relationships. In a one-to-one relationship, one record in a table is related to one (and only one) record in another table. An example of this type of relationship can commonly be found in the design of personnel tracking databases, where employee medical coverage is typically tracked in a table separate from employee office locations. One table may contain the office location and phone extension for an employee, and another table may contain the health provider name and the annual cost of the medical plan for which the employee is a subscriber. Each table will contain one record for a given employee, and the tables will be linked on a common field (such as an employee ID number or a social security number). In this case, a one-to-one relationship exists between the tables.

Also less common than the one-to-many relationship (and by nature more complex) is the *many-to-many* relationship. In this type of relationship, one or more records in one table are related to one or more records in another table. A common example (often used to teach the basics of database design) involves classes and students at any college. A database designed to track classes and students at a small college could have a table named Classes, and a table named Students. A record within the Classes table representing any single class would be related to a number of students; correspondingly, a record within the Students table representing a particular student would be related to any number of classes. In such a case, a many-to-many relationship exists between the Students table and the Classes table. Access does not directly support the creation of this type of relationship, but it can be implemented with the use of an intermediate, or "linking" table between the two tables containing the "many" records.

In Access, you can establish relationships at the database level to support the design of your relational queries, forms, and reports. You do so by means of the Relationship Tools area of the ribbon bar. Once you establish relationships in Access, the relationships are automatically used to link fields in any queries, forms, and reports that include multiple tables within their design. While you aren't required to use this feature to establish relationships (you can just design relational queries instead), it can be a significant time-saver, as it simplifies the design of any relational forms or reports within your application.

A second advantage of establishing relationships between tables in Access is that it enables the use of *referential integrity*. Referential integrity is a process by which Access automatically protects the data within your related tables from certain changes or deletions that would break the relationship between records. For example, with referential integrity enabled, you could not delete a given client from the Clients table in the example described previously without deleting all the corresponding calls for that client. And Access would not allow you to add a record to the Calls table containing a client ID number that does not exist in the Clients table. In Access, you can see any relationships that have been established at the database level in the Relationships window, an example of which appears later in this chapter, in Figure 18. To view this window, click the Database Tools tab, then click the Relationship Tools icon in the ribbon bar.

In your database, you can establish relationships at the database level with these steps:

1. With all tables visible in the Navigation Pane, click the Relationship Tools icon in the ribbon bar. When establishing relationships at the database level for the first time, an empty window appears with the Show Table dialog box, as shown in Figure 15.

Figure 15 The Show Tables dialog box

2. In the Show Tables dialog box, click the Tables tab to see all tables in the database, or click the Queries tab

to see all queries in the database. To see both tables and queries simultaneously, click the Both tab.

3. Select the table or query that you want to add to the relationship, and click the Add button. (Alternately, you can just double-click the desired table or query.)

4. Repeat step 3 for every table or query that is to be added to the Relationships window. (The order in which the tables or queries is selected does not matter.) When done, click Close.

5. Next, create the links between the common fields of the tables (or queries) that form the relationships, by dragging the field from the primary table (or query) to the matching field of the related table (or query). When you drag and drop a field, the Edit Relationships dialog box appears, as shown in Figure 16.

Figure 16 The Edit Relationships dialog box

6. If necessary, you can change the fields that Access suggests in the Edit Relationships dialog box as the basis for the link between the related tables or queries. Access makes its best guess as to the proper field and that guess is generally, but not always, correct. While fields used to link tables do not need to have the same name, they must be of the same type, with the exception of AutoNumber fields which can be linked to Number fields.)

7. If you wish to enable referential integrity, turn on the Enforce Referential Integrity check box. With the check

41

box turned on, you can also enable the Cascade Update Related Fields and Cascade Delete Related Fields options, if desired. (With Cascade Update Related Fields turned on, any changes made to a primary key of the parent table or query are automatically updated in the foreign key fields for all related records in the child table or query. With Cascade Delete Related Records turned on, if a record is deleted in the parent table or query, all related records matching that record's primary key in the child table are automatically deleted.)

8. If the relationship type shown at the bottom of the Edit Relationships dialog box is not the type that you prefer, click the Join Type button to display the Join Properties dialog box (Figure 17). In this dialog box, you can select the desired type of join (one to one or one to many) by clicking the desired option. In most cases, you will want a one to many relationship. When done, click Close to put away this dialog box

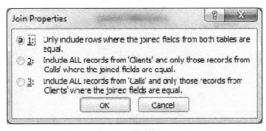

Figure 17 The Join Properties dialog box

9. Click the Create button in the Edit Relationships dialog box to create the relationship. When you do this, a line appears between the tables indicating the type of relationship that exists between the tables, where the numeral "1" indicates a "one" side and the infinity symbol indicates a "many" side.

10. Repeat steps 5-9 for every relationship that you want to add between tables (or queries), and close the Relationships window. When Access asks if you wish to save the changes to the Relationships window, click Yes. In

some cases, relationships can appear quite complex, depending on the number of tables and the overall level of complexity of your application. An excellent example of this is the Northwind Traders 2007 sample database that can be downloaded for free at Office.com, which contains numerous related tables. Figure 18 shows the Relationships window for the Northwind Traders database.

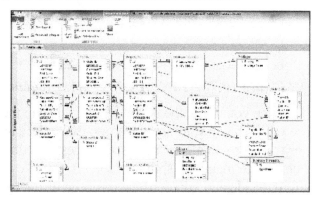

Figure 18 The Relationships window for the Northwind Traders database

If the process of *normalizing* the design of a database (eliminating redundant data and choosing appropriate relationships) is new to you, Access offers help in the form of the Table Analyzer Wizard. The Table Analyzer Wizard analyzes your existing tables (they must contain data), and makes recommendations as to how your data can be properly split into multiple tables. For this analysis to work correctly, the table must contain at least three records of actual data.

To start the wizard, click the Database Tools icon in the ribbon bar, then click Analyze Table. After clicking Next twice to bypass explanatory screens about how the Table Analyzer works, you will be asked to select the table that the wizard should split into multiple related tables (Figure 19).

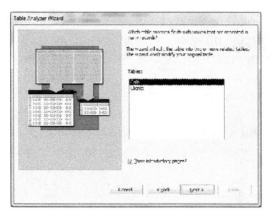

Figure 19 The Table Analyzer Wizard dialog box

Once you select the desired table, you can then choose whether you want the wizard to make decisions for you, or whether you just want to see suggestions that you can later use to manually split the table. If you allow the wizard to decide and you don't care for the results, you can use the Back button to go back and make your own decision as to where the table should be split.

Once you are satisfied with the design of your tables and you have created the accompanying queries, forms, and reports needed, you can use the design techniques outlined in this briefing to construct a complete application.

Chapter 5 - Fast Application Development with the Command Button Wizard

The hands-on example described previously makes use of a useful timesaving tool in the hands of any Access developer, the *Command Button Wizard.* As you build forms that are a part of your user interface, you can use the Command Button Wizard to add buttons that perform common user tasks, such as navigating within a table, opening forms on demand, adding and editing records, and printing reports. And since the Command Button Wizard operates by adding VBA code appropriate to the task to the design of the button, you can use the buttons as a starting point and make additional modifications to the VBA code (assuming you are familiar with programming using VBA, Visual Basic for Applications). As an example, Figure 20 shows a form containing a variety of buttons, all created with the aid of the Command Button Wizard.

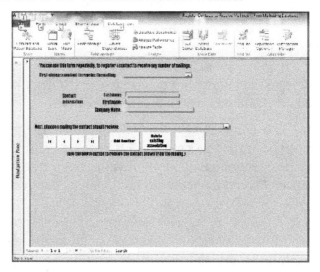

Figure 20 A form containing buttons created with the Command Button Wizard

You can create command buttons using the Command Button Wizard with these steps:

1. Open the appropriate form in Design view.

2. In the ribbon bar, click the Command Button tool to select it.

3. In the form, click at the location where you wish to place the button.

4. In the first Command Button Wizard dialog box, under Categories, select the desired category to reveal the actions that apply to that particular category. Under Actions, select the action that you want the button to perform, then click Next.

5. In the next dialog box that appears, enable the Text or Picture option button, as desired. If you choose Text, you can then enter text into the accompanying text box, and that text appears on the face of the button. If you choose Picture, you can then choose from a list of available graphics to place on the face of the button.

6. Click Next to proceed to the final dialog box of the Command Button Wizard. In this dialog box, you can enter a name that will be used by the VBA code which is attached to the button, or you can accept the default shown. When done, click Finish to create the button.

The Command Button Wizard can be used to create buttons performing tasks that fall into six overall categories: record navigation (previous, next, first, last, and find record); record operations (add, delete, duplicate, print, and save record); form operations (apply filter, edit filter, open form, close form, print form, print current form, and refresh form data); report operations (mail report, preview report, print report, and send report to file); application (quit application, run application, run Excel, run Word, and run Notepad); and Miscellaneous (auto dialer, print table, run macro, and run query).

With a working familiarity of VBA programming, you can modify the buttons to perform additional tasks, or you can create command buttons that perform your own very specialized tasks. With the form open in Design view, right-click on any command button, and choose Build Event from the menu that appears. The code for the button appears in a Visual Basic editor window, similar to the example shown in Figure 21.

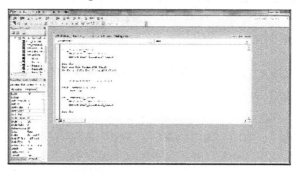

Figure 21 An example of VBA code used by a command button

You can modify the code as desired, and close the VBA editor window to save the changes. And often, the necessary modifications are simple in nature. For example, you might choose 'Record Operations' followed by 'Add New Record' in the wizard to add a button to a form that allows the user to easily add a new record to a table. The button created by the wizard to perform such a task would contain the following line of VBA code to actually create the new record:

DoCmd.GoToRecord , , acNewRec

If the users (who are adding hundreds of new records each day) state that a nice improvement would consist of automatically moving the insertion pointer to a field called 'Lastname' after the new record was added, you could easily accommodate that request by adding an additional line of VBA code to the code already stored in the On Click property for the button. The program code that performs the work of adding the record and moving the insertion pointer to the desired field would then resemble the following:

DoCmd.GoToRecord , , acNewRec

Me!Lastname.SetFocus

While programming in VBA is a subject that is beyond the scope of this article, modifying the code that is created by the Command Button Wizards can be an excellent way to learn the basics of VBA programming.

Setting the Access Options for Your Application

As part of any application, you'll need to decide whether to use a 'home screen' style of form as the first form that the user sees, or whether to use a form containing data as a data-based starting point for the application. The first approach generally makes sense when an application has a number of tables, and no single table is used more extensively than the others. On the other hand, if one particular table serves as the basis for your application, it may make sense to initially present that form to the user, and to add command buttons as needed to that form, to allow the users to perform related tasks. The Northwind Traders form that appears once a user logs into the database is an excellent example of this type of form, and is shown in Figure 22.

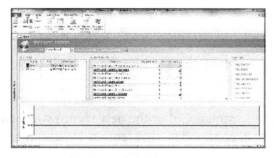

Figure 22 An Access data form that serves as the starting point for an application

Once you've decided on the initial form that should be seen by the users, you'll need to set the options for the database to load that form. And you can use the same options to hide the Navigation Pane and to turn off default menus or toolbars as desired, to keep your users from getting into trouble by wandering into places where they have no business being. You can do this with the options shown in the Access Options dialog box (Figure 23). Open the database, then under the File menu, under Help, click Options. Next, choose Current Database in the Access Options dialog box that appears.

Figure 23 The Access Options dialog box

In the Display Form list box, you choose the form that you want to initially display to your end users. (The list shows all forms that are stored in the database.) Additionally, you will probably want to hide the Navigation Pane when the application starts. To do so, turn off the check box for the Display Navigation Pane option. If you want to disable the default Access menus or toolbars, you can turn off the Allow Full Menus and/or the Allow

Built-In Toolbars options. (You may need to scroll down in the dialog box to see all of these options.)

And if you wish to hide the default shortcut menus that Access normally provides for forms and reports, turn off the Allow Default Shortcut Menus option. (If you hide the default Access menus from your users, be sure to provide them with sufficient options, such as command buttons, to perform all necessary tasks.)

In the Application Title text box, you can enter an optional title for the application; any title you enter replaces the default phrase of 'Microsoft Access' that normally appears in the title bar of the application window.

Remember that once you have set a default startup form in the Display Form/Page list box, the chosen form always appears whenever the database is opened in Access. If you want to work on the design of any database objects and cancel the loading of the initial form, you can do so by holding the Shift key depressed as you open the database.

Chapter 6 - Putting It All Together

This chapter covers a number of closing points that will help you put the professional finishing touches on your custom Access application. Included in these topics are how you can create ways for users of your application to navigate between the forms of an application; how you can ask users for information and act on their responses; and how to provide help screens so that your users know exactly what is going on at any point within the application.

Navigating Between Forms of an Application

With custom applications of any complexity, you are likely to deal with a number of forms. And within your forms used for data entry and editing, you may have a sizable number of controls. Navigation, both within an individual form and from one form to another, is one important aspect of custom application design in Access.

When it comes to navigation within a data entry form, you can use various properties that are a part of the form's design. Open the form in Design view, right-click any control that is associated with a field of a table, choose Properties from the pop-up men to open the Property Sheet for the control, and click the Other tab. Under this tab, you will see the Auto Tab, Tab Stop, and Tab Index properties (Figure 24).

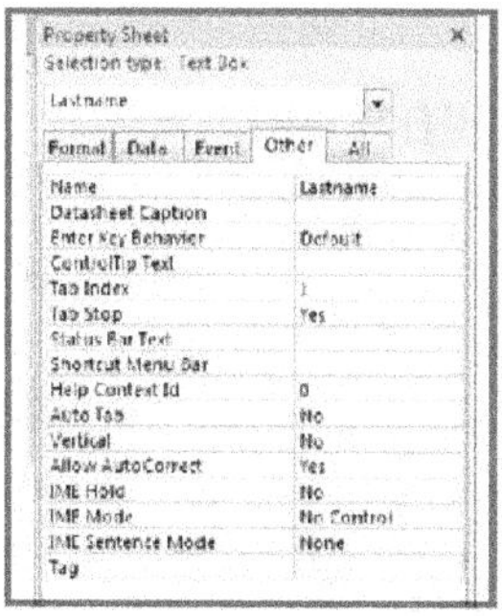

Figure 24 The Property Sheet for a text box control

You can use the Auto Tab property to determine whether the insertion pointer moves to the next control (field) when characters that a user types fill the field. If you set this property to Yes, when a user fills a control, a Tab character is automatically generated, causing the insertion pointer to move to the next control. For ease of use, you may want to set this property to Yes if you have fields that always fill with the same number of characters (such as a Zip Code field).

You can use the Tab Stop property under control of VBA program code to enable (or disable) the ability of the insertion pointer to move to a control on a form. As an example, if a personnel form contained a list box with choices of Single or Married, and the user selected Single, there would be no need to force the user to move through an adjacent field for Spouse Name. Assuming a working knowledge of VBA, you can use code to set the Tab Stop property to No when you want to disable a control.

The Tab Index property determines where a control falls in the order of all controls throughout the form, beginning with the numeral zero. Hence, a control having a Tab Index setting of 5 would be the sixth control reached as the user repeatedly presses the Tab key (the first control on the form has a Tab Index setting of zero). You can change this value as needed to change the order which the insertion pointer follows as it moves through the form when the Tab key is pressed.

For navigation between different forms of an application, you can use command buttons, placed on forms with the aid of the Command Button Wizard, to place buttons on forms that call other forms. For ease of use, a Close Form button should be included on all forms used for data entry or editing, as the default Windows Close icon may not be an intuitive choice to untrained users.

If you have an application that presents a large number of available forms to users for a variety of tasks, you may want to consider the technique of loading all required forms with a macro when the application starts, then alternately hiding or displaying the forms by means of VBA code as they are needed by users. To hide the forms as they are loaded, you can set the Visible property of each form to 'No' (or, False). Then, in the Click event for each command button that displays a form, you can use VBA code to set the form's Visible property to True. In such a case, the VBA code for a button that displays a form named 'ClientsForm' might resemble the following:

```
Sub ClientsButton_Click

    Forms!ClientsForm.Visible = True

End Sub
```

And a 'Close Form' button on the same form might contain code attached to the button that resembles the following:

```
Sub CloseButton_Click

    Forms!ClientsForm.Visible = False

End Sub
```

The drawback to this approach (in addition to requiring a minimal familiarity with VBA programming) is that the application takes longer to load, because all the forms must be loaded before the user can begin using the system. The advantage to this approach is that once the application does load, users move between forms with minimal delay, as the forms do not need to be loaded into memory each time that they are opened.

Displaying Message Boxes with Macros or VBA

Often during the design of an application's user interface, you will encounter a need to present some sort of an informational message to the user. You can do this by means of a macro, or (if you are familiar with VBA programming) by means of a small amount of VBA program code. If the message needs to be presented as a part of a process (such as printing a report or exporting a file), it is often easier to use a macro, and include the display of the message along with the other needed tasks as part of the design of the macro. In the Action column of the new macro, choose MsgBox; then, under Action Arguments, type the desired message that you want to present to the user into the Message text box. (Successive rows of the macro can contain actions to perform other tasks.) As an example, the macro shown in Figure 25 displays a message box asking the user to insert a blank CD, before performing an export action of data to an Excel spreadsheet.

Figure 25 A macro that displays a message box

When you use a macro in this manner, you can force a command button on a form to run the macro, by choosing Miscellaneous followed by Run Macro in the Command Button Wizard dialog box.

Experienced VBA programmers can use the MsgBox function to accomplish the same result of presenting a message to the user. Using the syntax of-

MsgBox("*message-text*")

as part of a VBA routine results in the display of a dialog box containing the text of the message, along with an OK button.

Getting Input for Programming Tasks

When you are resorting to VBA in order to perform certain tasks within an application, you may need to prompt users for specific information, and use that information elsewhere. To do this, you can make use of the InputBox function. Unlike the MsgBox function, which only displays a message, the InputBox function can display a message *and* obtain a value from the user. The InputBox function displays a message within a dialog box, and the dialog box contains a text box, along with OK and Cancel buttons. When the user enters a response in the text box and clicks OK, the function returns the value that was typed into the text box. In your VBA code, you use the following format:

Variable-name = InputBox("*message-to-user*" , "*title*")

And the text that you enter for "title" appears in the title bar of the dialog box. As an example, the dialog box shown in Figure 26 could be displayed using the following VBA code:

TheAnswer = InputBox("Enter employee ID number:","Find employee")

55

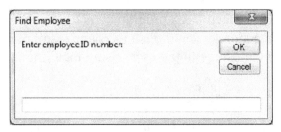

***Figure 26 A dialog box created with the InputBox
function***

Once the user enters a value in the text box and
clicks OK, that value is assigned to the variable name on
the left side of the equal symbol. (Note that if the user
clicks Cancel, a zero-length text string ("") gets returned by
the VBA code.

Providing Users with Help

One sign of a professional application is the
inclusion of help screens to assist the user with specific
tasks. And you can easily meet this need, by designing
forms that contain large amounts of explanatory text. You
can build help text into a series of forms that contain just
the help text and a Close Form button. When in Design
view for the form, add a Label control for each paragraph
of text, and size the label large enough to display the full
text of the paragraph. On the data entry forms or 'home
screen' forms of your application where the help is needed,
use the Command Button Wizard to add a button with a
caption such as 'Help' or 'Click for Help'. And have the
button open the appropriate form containing the help text.
Figure 27 shows a help screen implemented using this
technique.

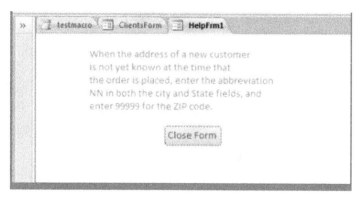

Figure 27 A sample of a help screen within an Access application

Creating a Shortcut to Launch the Application

One final touch you'll want to provide users with is a simple way to launch the application. You can do this by creating a Windows shortcut to the database (.ACCDB) file. First, store the database file on a shared network drive that is accessible to all intended users of the application. Next, locate the database file using Windows Explorer, right-click the file, and choose Create Shortcut from the menu that appears. When the shortcut appears under a new name within Windows Explorer, drag the shortcut onto your desktop. You can then rename the shortcut to an appropriate name, right click the shortcut, and choose 'Send To/Mail Recipient' from the menu to e-mail the shortcut to your network users. Upon receiving the e-mail, they can drag the attachment onto their desktop, and double-click it to launch the application.

Chapter 7 - Recommendations for User Interface Design

Since Access forms make up the heart of your user interface, there are a number of aspects of good applications design that you should keep in mind as you build any Access application.

Ensure that data entry follows a logical format. Based on the way that language is implemented in the Western world, our eyes follow a logical sequence of left to right and top to bottom when reading printed information. You should design your forms with these natural tendencies in mind. When a new form opens, a user's eyes will tend to focus on the upper-left corner of the screen and continue reading from that point, so your text and fields that indicate a logical starting point should flow from that area downwards.

Avoiding overcrowding data entry forms. If you develop any number of applications, you'll often encounter situations where you need to present users with a large number of fields. You should avoid the inexperienced developer's tendency to crowd a large number of fields onto a single form, as users will find such forms visually confusing and difficult to use. Also, try to leave sufficient amounts of "white space", or unoccupied areas, near the borders of the form. Forms that are designed with insufficient white space appear overly busy or visually confusing.

Traditionally, fields and their accompanying labels are placed in a column, flush left. If you have too many fields to comfortably fit at the left side of a single form, you can opt to have two columns (assuming that the fields are not extremely wide). In many cases, you will need to design your application so that data entry is performed by means of multiple forms, and a command button on one form can open another form when needed. Another option

59

when dealing with a large number of fields is to make use of *tabbed forms*. While in Design view for a form, you can use the Tab control to place a tabbed form within a form. You can then group your fields on the different tabs of the form. One disadvantage of this approach is that tabbed forms cannot be created with the aid of the Form Wizards. Therefore, you will need to learn the nuts and bolts of manually designing forms if you wish to make use of tabbed forms. Figure 28 shows an example of a tabbed form within Access.

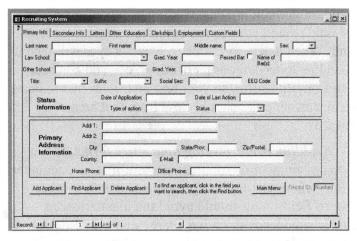

Figure 28 An example of a tabbed form

If you aren't familiar with the use of tabbed forms, you can use these steps to create a tabbed form:

1. Begin creating a new form manually, without the aid of the Form Wizards.

2. In the menu area, under Form Design Tools, click Design.

3. In the ribbon bar, locate the Tab control (it's the icon resembling a tabbed file folder), and click it.

4. In the form, click where you wish to place the upper-left corner of the Tab control, and drag to the desired lower-right corner for the control. When you release the

60

mouse, Access creates a tabbed control with two tabs, like the example shown in Figure 29.

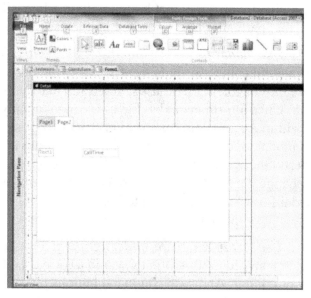

Figure 29 A tabbed form in Design view

4. To change the name of a tab, double-click the tab to open its Property Sheet, click the Property Sheet's Format tab, and enter a desired name in the Caption text box.

5. To add more tabs, right-click the tab that a new tab should appear after, and then choose Insert Page from the menus.

6. To add your desired controls to each tab, select the tab, drag the desired control type (such as a text box) to the desired location on the tab, and set the control's properties so that the control is associated with the desired field.

You can use other techniques of manual form design in Access to add other types of controls, text labels, or graphics to any of the tabs of the form. And keep one design hint in mind when designing tabbed forms: if you want to add command buttons that should be visible when any tab is selected, place these buttons on the form outside the border of the tab control. If you place a command button directly on a tab, that button will only be visible when that particular tab is selected by the user.

Use modal forms for important data entry. Where users should complete all data entry in a particular form before moving on to other tasks, you can make the form *modal*. Once a form is modal, the user cannot do anything else within Access until that form is closed. To make a form modal, open the form in Design view, bring up the Property Sheet, click the Other tab in the Property Sheet, and change the Modal property to Yes. (If you make a form a modal form, it is a wise idea to include a Cancel button, so users have the option of changing their minds.)

Use text as an aid to understanding. Text labels should clearly identify all fields within a form used for data entry or editing. And with command buttons placed on forms, you will need to decide whether graphic images on the buttons can be easily understood, or whether text captions are necessary. How much additional text may be needed in a form will depend on what you want the form to accomplish. But in nearly all cases, you should follow standard use of capitalization (only the initial letter in a phrase should be upper-case). Readability studies have proven that text composed of all uppercase letters is more difficult to read than text that is composed in a normal fashion.

Use clear, understandable graphics on command buttons. While on the topic of command buttons used on forms, resist the urge to place certain graphics on buttons simply because they 'look cute' to you, the developer. If you decide to use graphics (as opposed to text captions) on your command buttons, think about whether the meaning of the graphic image will be easily understood by a wide variety of users. If you think that any doubt may arise as to the purpose of the buttons, consider adding Control Tips text as help. (To do this, right-click the button while in Design view, choose Properties from the menu, click the Other tab in the Properties Sheet, and enter the help text in the Control Tip text box. The help text then appears when the user holds the mouse pointer stationary over the control.)

Avoid unnecessary graphics. With modern Windows-based PCs, graphics are understandably popular. However, overuse of unneeded graphics can turn your Access application into a slow resource hog. Avoid the use of decorative images or detailed corporate logos, especially if you know that the users' hardware is not up to par. Overly flashy forms that you design may load and run fine on your high-end development system, but if the people down in the mailroom using the application are stuck with hardware that will barely run the current version of Windows, they will be frustrated with Access forms that take an interminably long time to load.

Use the variety of form controls to your best advantage. Fields on data entry forms are most often used to store text, but you are by no means limited to text boxes for all of your controls that are linked to the fields of a table. Access forms offer a variety of control types, including list boxes, combo boxes, check boxes, and option buttons. And the Control Wizards that are a tool of form design make it easy to work with these types of controls. For example, if a user can enter a limited number of possible entries in a field, don't use a text box; use a combo box instead. Logical (Yes/No) fields on forms should make use of check boxes. Such design techniques improve the appearance of your forms and reduce possible data entry errors.

Don't overdo the use of colors. Color can be a useful aid under some circumstances; for example, you might want to highlight a particular group of fields on a form with a rectangular red border to draw attention to the need to fill in those fields. But you should avoid any temptation to add large numbers of varying colors for no good reason. Techniques of sensible application design avoid the use of more than two contrasting colors on any single form.

Finally, if your application is a complex one, consider the many ways in which you can provide help to users at any potentially confusing point in the process. When designing forms, you can use the Status Bar property of a control to specify text that will appear in the status bar (at the bottom of the screen) whenever the user moves to that control. And the help screen techniques discussed earlier in this article can be used to provide screens containing explanatory help where needed.

Summary

This book has covered how you can use the design techniques that are a part of Access to create a database application that novice users will find easy to use. Access provides the tools you need to combine tables, queries, forms, reports, and macros into an integrated application that will be simple for relatively untrained users to work with. And in the long run, helping your users accomplish their jobs with a minimal amount of strain is the goal of technology.

To visit the author's Amazon page for a complete list of additional books by the author, visit the following Amazon Author page:

http://www.amazon.com/author/edwardjones_writer

Alternately, you may visit the author's web site at:

http://www.thekindlewizard.com

Creating Applications with Microsoft Access 2010

By Edward C. Jones

Revised (print) edition copyright June 16, 2014 –

Edward C Jones, Jones-Mack Technical Services, Charlotte, NC 28205

www.ingramcontent.com/pod-product-compliance
Lightning Source LLC
Chambersburg PA
CBHW061034050326
40689CB00012B/2811